The Gunpowder Plot

Rob Lloyd Jones

Illustrated by Daniele Dickmann

Reading consultant: Alison Kelly

Contents

This story is about a clash between two religions – Protestantism and Catholicism. Protestants rejected the Catholic Church, claiming it was rich and corrupt. England was once a Catholic nation, but switched to Protestantism. Some people hoped to change things back, however they could…

Chapter 1

Religious change

"Open up, by order of the King!"
The soldier thumped on the
monastery door until a bolt slid
and the door creaked open. He
shoved aside a terrified monk as
troops stormed into the monastery.

3

It was 1536 and the Pope – the head of the Catholic Church in Rome – had refused to grant King Henry VIII a divorce. Furious, Henry had declared himself the Supreme Head of the Church of England.

Henry's soldiers looted Catholic monasteries and arrested monks. Now that the King had rejected the Pope, a new form of Christianity became popular in England – Protestantism.

No one knew it then, but this change would eventually lead to a sensational plot to kill every member of the country's government...

Henry's daughter, Mary I, made the Pope the head of the English church again – and had around 300 Protestants burned at the stake.

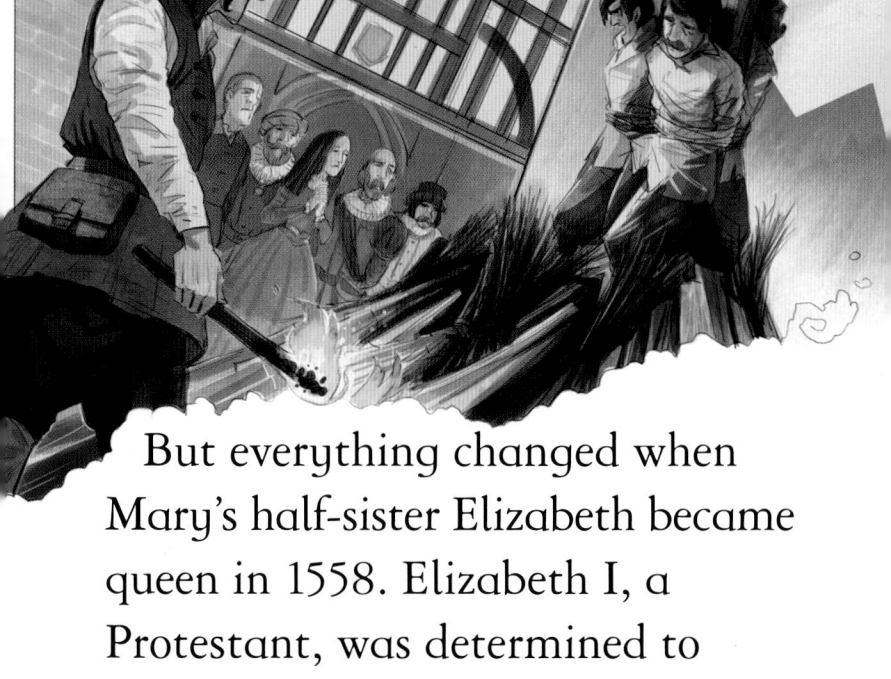

But everything changed when Mary's half-sister Elizabeth became queen in 1558. Elizabeth I, a Protestant, was determined to stamp out Catholicism in England once and for all.

Catholics were forced to pay fines and banned from holding religious services. Many still worshipped but in secret.

Catholic priests visited nobles' mansions. If soldiers came to hunt them, they scrambled into secret hiding places known as priest holes.

In 1586, Elizabeth's spies uncovered a plot led by a group of Catholic nobles, to kill the Queen and replace her with her cousin – the Catholic Scottish ruler, Mary Queen of Scots. The plotters were dragged to the Tower of London, tortured and executed.

Elizabeth was convinced that other Catholics might have the same plan. So, in February 1587, she had Mary Queen of Scots – her own cousin – executed.

Gradually the Catholic faith was being put down. But, still, some nobles dreamed of England becoming Catholic again. They whispered and they plotted...

Chapter 2

New hope?

In 1603, the hopes of English Catholics were raised again. Queen Elizabeth had died. The new king, James I, was Protestant but his wife was Catholic – and he was the son of Mary Queen of Scots. Catholics hoped they might at last be allowed to worship freely.

But that same year a Catholic plot was discovered against the King. Encouraged by Protestant advisors, King James announced his 'utter detestation' of Catholics. Anyone who didn't attend Protestant church services was fined.

A year later things grew even more frustrating. In 1604, England agreed a peace treaty with Catholic Spain.

English Catholics hoped the Spanish king would demand better treatment for them but they weren't mentioned in the treaty at all.

One Catholic noble decided it was time to take action.

Like many Catholics, Robert Catesby – a handsome gentleman from Warwickshire – worshipped at home in secret. Unlike most others, he began to plot against the King.

Catesby wanted to kill King James
but his plot was bigger than that.
He planned to strike during a
ceremony in which the King 'opened'
the Houses of Parliament – the home
of the English government, in London.

14

As well as the King, Protestant bishops would be at the ceremony, and almost every member of Parliament. With enough gunpowder Catesby could blow them all to smithereens.

The date of the ceremony was set for October 3, 1605. There was time to prepare but Catesby needed help. He approached three trusted Catholic friends – Thomas Wintour, Jack Wright and Thomas Percy.

Unfortunately none of the group knew how to use gunpowder. They needed more help.

Thomas Wintour set off for the Netherlands, where he met with an English Catholic soldier named Guy Fawkes.

Fawkes, an expert at using gunpowder, was intrigued by Wintour's hints about Catesby's plot. He returned to England to hear more.

On May 20, 1604, the five plotters met at the Duck and Drake, a rowdy tavern in the middle of London. They all knew that even talking about plotting against the King could be punished with death.

They booked a private room, so no one else would hear their plans. Then, one by one, each man placed a hand on a prayer book and swore an oath of secrecy. They began to talk in hushed voices. They had a king to kill and a lot to plan.

Chapter 3

Guy Fawkes

The Houses of Parliament, in Westminster, were a sprawling mass of buildings. Some were the remains of an old royal palace: chapels, chambers and law courts. Others were lodging houses, taverns, shops or storerooms.

It was a busy, bustling place, where traders, lawyers and nobles came and went.

Somehow the plotters needed to hide gunpowder – a *lot* of gunpowder – underneath the House of Lords, the chamber in the Houses of Parliament where the opening ceremony would be held.

It would be tricky for Catesby's gang to smuggle barrels of gunpowder into Westminster. Most of them were known Catholic rebels, watched by government spies.

Guy Fawkes though was less well known. He had only recently returned from Europe, where he'd been fighting for the Spanish against the Dutch, so he could visit Westminster without suspicion.

The plotters rented a house
on the south bank of the River
Thames to store supplies, as well
as a house next to the House of
Lords, in Westminster.

Guy Fawkes moved into the Westminster house, pretending to be a servant called John Johnson. At night he rowed across the Thames, sneaking barrels of gunpowder from one hideout to the other.

Catesby gathered more help as well, and the number of plotters grew to ten. The gang began to dig a tunnel from their Westminster house to under the House of Lords, and fill it with gunpowder.

In March 1605, a better option came up when Thomas Percy rented a ground floor cellar directly beneath the House of Lords.

The cellar was dark and filthy, but perfect for their plan. Now they didn't need a tunnel.

Chapter 4

Final plans

In July, an outbreak of plague in London forced the plotters to change their plan again. It was too dangerous for the government to meet in October, so a new date was set for the Opening of Parliament – November 5.

The plotters had more time to prepare but also to worry. Some of them grew concerned for the Catholic nobles who would be killed at the ceremony. They wanted to warn them but Catesby refused to allow it. No one else could know.

One of the plotters didn't listen.

On the night of October 26, an anonymous letter arrived at the house of Lord Monteagle, a Catholic nobleman. It warned him to avoid the opening ceremony, when Parliament would receive 'a terrible blow'.

Monteagle climbed onto his horse and raced to Westminster. He handed the letter to Robert Cecil, the Earl of Salisbury, who was in charge of the King's security.

Salisbury was a clever, calculating man who hated Catholics. He decided to wait and catch the plotters red handed...

By November 4, there were 36 barrels of gunpowder in the cellar, covered by bundles of sticks and heaps of coal. Everything now relied on Guy Fawkes.

As Fawkes carefully laid a gunpowder trail, which he would light to set off the explosion, the rest of the gang rode north. As soon as the King was dead, they planned to gather an army of Catholic nobles and start a rebellion.

That night, Fawkes hid in the cold cellar. He was wrapped in a thick coat but still his lantern trembled in his hand, casting shadows around the arched walls.

His horse was tied up outside, and he wore spurs on his boots. He was ready for a quick getaway.

Then, around midnight, he heard a noise. Footsteps!

They were marching closer. Had he been discovered? Fawkes rushed for the cellar door but it was too late.

Led by a noble named Sir Thomas Knyvett and his associate Edmund Doubleday, a troop of soldiers stormed into the cellar.

"Surrender!" Doubleday barked.

Fawkes wasn't giving up without a fight. He charged at the doorway, grabbing Doubleday's arm to force him out of the way. Doubleday drew a dagger from his belt but before he could use it, guards pounced on Fawkes.

Fawkes kicked and screamed as the soldiers pinned him roughly to the ground.

"Get this traitor out of here," Knyvett ordered.

Chapter 5

On the run

On November 5, Guy Fawkes was dragged before the king he had tried to kill. He refused to name the other plotters. Instead he snarled at James, admitting that he had planned to blow him up and wished that he'd succeeded.

King James was impressed with
Fawkes' courage. Still, he ordered
the defiant prisoner to be taken
away and tortured.

Fawkes was taken to the Tower of London and tortured for two terrible days. He was put on the rack, a grisly device that stretched its victim's body.

Finally, on November 7, Fawkes gave up the names of his gang and signed a confession.

By then he was a broken man, shaking so hard that he could barely hold the quill.

The rest of the plotters were now on the run. Led by Catesby, several of the gang reached Warwick Castle, where they stole horses and rode further north to Staffordshire.

The gang hoped to find help from Catholic nobles but no one would take them in now that they were wanted men.

Eight of the gang hid in Holbeche House, the home of a plotter named Stephen Littleton.

They were being hunted by soldiers and they had nowhere to run. Instead they decided to stand their ground.

That night, they prepared to fight, gathering all their weapons.

What little gunpowder they had was damp, so the plotters laid it by the fire to dry. It was a bad idea — a spark from the fire lit the powder. The explosion injured several of the gang and left one of them blind.

By the morning of November 8, Holbeche House was surrounded by 200 soldiers.

Muskets fired and windows shattered. Four of the gang, including Catesby and Percy, died in the shoot out. Three others were captured. At the same time, soldiers rounded up the rest of the gang across the country.

The plotters were locked in the Tower of London, where one of them died. On January 27, 1606, the rest were taken to Westminster Hall, part of the Houses of Parliament, for their trial.

Spectators crammed in, eager to catch a glimpse of the plotters who were now famous.

All of the plotters were found guilty of treason. Some accepted their fate. Others begged for mercy. But there was none. The sentence was death, in the most painful way possible...

Chapter 6

Hanged, drawn and quartered

On the chilly morning of January 30, crowds gathered in the churchyard of St. Paul's Cathedral. They whispered excitedly, rising to tiptoes and jostling for a better view of the hanging scaffold.

Four of the remaining plotters
arrived for their execution, dragged
on ropes behind horses. The next
day the other four, including Guy
Fawkes, were executed outside
Westminster Hall.

Their sentence was to be hanged, and then cut down alive, tortured and cut into four pieces.

The crowd watched as Guy Fawkes was led, shaking and weak, onto the scaffold.

Fawkes was hanged but before he could be taken down for torture, his neck had already broken. He was dead.

He escaped the misery of being 'hanged, drawn and quartered'. The other plotters did not.

The heads of the leaders, Robert Catesby and Thomas Percy, were stuck on spikes and displayed at the Houses of Parliament. They were grisly warnings to anyone else who dared plot against the King.

Chapter 7

Remember, remember

After the Gunpowder Plot the government stamped down hard on Catholics. Priests thought to have helped the plotters went into hiding, although they were later captured and arrested. New laws stopped Catholics from doing certain jobs, or voting in elections.

In 1606, a law was passed
making November 5 an official
day to remember the failure of
the plot. Church bells rang and
bonfires were lit.

The celebrations have remained part of English tradition ever since. Every November 5, all over England, the night sky is lit up by dazzling firework displays.

Although the plot was led by Robert Catesby, Guy Fawkes is remembered as its chief villain. Children make model 'guys' to burn on bonfires, and they chant the popular rhyme:

Remember, remember the fifth of November,
Gunpowder, treason and plot.
I see no reason why gunpowder treason
Should ever be forgot.

Timeline of the Gunpowder Plot

1603

24 March

James I is crowned King of England. Soon after, he introduces fines against anyone who doesn't attend Protestant services.

December

The plotters begin to dig a tunnel to the House of Lords.

24 May

Thomas Percy rents a house near Parliament.

1605

March

The plotters rent a cellar beneath the House of Lords.

March to October

Guy Fawkes smuggles barrels of gunpowder into the cellar.

8 November

1606

Several plotters are captured at Holbeche House. Catesby and Percy and the Wright brothers are killed.

27 January

The plotters go on trial at Westminster Hall.

30 January

Robert Wintour, Everard Digby, John Grant and Thomas Bates are hanged, drawn and quartered in St. Paul's Churchyard.

1604

April
Robert Catesby tells Thomas Wintour and Jack Wright of his plot.

Around Easter
Thomas Wintour meets Guy Fawkes in the Netherlands.

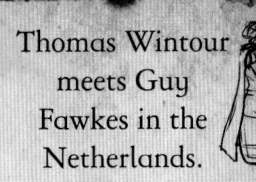

20 May

Robert Catesby, Guy Fawkes, Thomas Wintour, Jack Wright and Thomas Percy meet at the Duck and Drake Inn.

26 October
Lord Monteagle receives a letter warning him not to attend the Opening of Parliament.

4 November
Soldiers search Parliament. They find gunpowder, and Guy Fawkes.

7 November
After two days of torture, Fawkes signs a confession.

31 January

Guy Fawkes, Thomas Wintour, Ambrose Rookwood and Robert Keyes are executed at Westminster.

Key people in the Gunpowder Plot

Robert Catesby devised
and led the plot.
He was shot and killed
at Holbeche House.

Guy Fawkes was captured
before lighting the fuse to 36
barrels of gunpowder beneath
Parliament. He was tortured
in the Tower of London and
executed in Westminster.

Thomas Wintour was
Robert Catesby's cousin
and recruited Guy Fawkes
in the Netherlands. He was
captured at Holbeche House
and executed in Westminster.

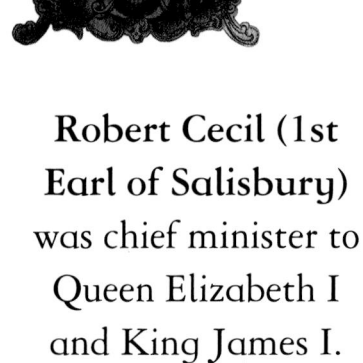

Francis Tresham probably sent the anonymous letter to Lord Monteagle. He was Monteagle's friend and brother-in-law.

Robert Cecil (1st Earl of Salisbury) was chief minister to Queen Elizabeth I and King James I.

James I was King of England from 1603 and King of Scotland (as James VI) from 1567. His 'utter detestation' of Catholics led to plots against his life.